Purple Martin

Robin

English Sparrow

Starling

Chimney Swift

Nighthawk

Pigeon

CITY BIRDS

CITY BIRDS

by Lucy and John Hawkinson

ALBERT WHITMAN AND COMPANY
Chicago, Illinois

CITY BIRDS

Birds live all around us in the city. They live on rooftops or in chimneys. They live under the eaves, or in the trees.

Some birds live in the city all year. Others visit only in the spring and summer. We cannot play with them or talk to them, but it is fun to watch the interesting things they do.

English sparrows are everywhere in the city. They are little gray-brown birds. They hop along beside you on a busy street. They come to your window sill for scraps of bread.

They play and fight in the city dust. When it rains, they splash around in puddles in the street.

Sometimes many sparrows meet on one tree. They chatter and make so much noise that it sounds like a party.

There are many pigeons in the city, too. They like the same places the sparrows do. But they are much bigger than sparrows, and they have brighter colored feathers to wear.

When something scares a flock of pigeons, they all fly up at once with a loud clapping of wings. They fly high above the buildings, and play follow the leader in the sky. When they fly down to the ground, they all land together in one spot.

The male pigeons are funny. They strut around
and puff out their chests to show off in front of
their mates. But their mates go right on eating,
and don't seem to notice them at all.

The black bird with a stumpy tail and long bill
is called a starling.

The starling is fast and graceful in the air, but
on the ground he is slow and clumsy. When he
walks he rocks from side to side, with his head
bent down.

You can see him perched on top of buildings or high in the trees in every part of the city. Even on cold winter days you can hear his odd song. He clucks, whistles and squeeks.

In the spring, he copies other birds' songs. He often fools people by sounding like a robin or a bluebird.

You can always find sparrows, pigeons and starlings in the city. They can be as much fun to watch as a policeman directing traffic, or a truck delivering coal.

Everyone is glad to see the first robin. After long winter months, it means that spring has come at last. The robin, with his bright colored breast and cheerful song, makes spring in the city a happy time.

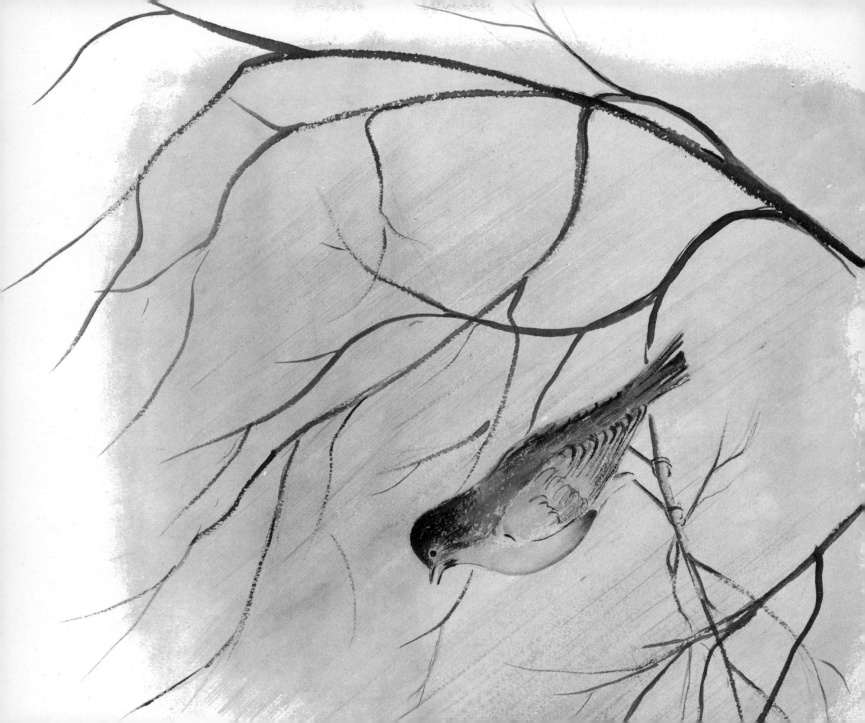

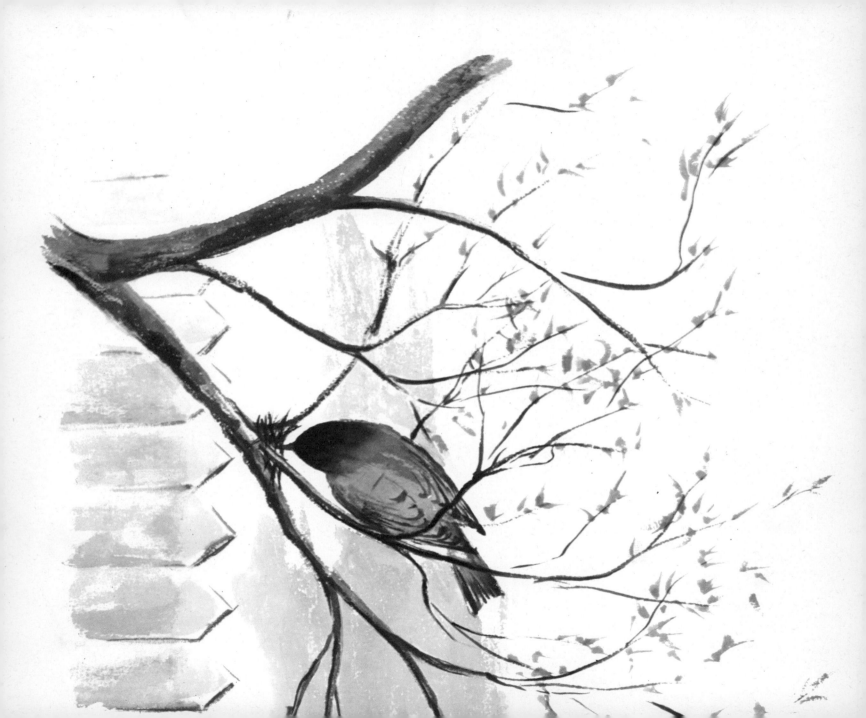

Robins have much work to do. They must dig for worms to eat. They must find a place to live. They must look for twigs to build their nests.

But no matter how busy they are, they still have time to sing their sweet song.

The first purple martins to come in the spring are the scouts. They fly ahead of the flock to find a place for them to live. Soon the rest of the martins come. They fill the city sky as they flutter and glide in long, sweeping curves.

The name, "purple martin", doesn't tell the bird's color. He is really a shiny dark blue.

Martins nest in houses that are put up by people in their back yards. The houses have many holes for the birds to go in to nest. Sometimes there are a dozen families living in one house, like people in an apartment building.

ST. THOMAS SCHOOL

On summer evenings you can hear the strange,
harsh call of the nighthawk. He is a slim, dark
bird. He has long, sharp wings.

The interesting thing about the nighthawk is the
way he dives. He dives straight down from high

above the rooftops. His wings are stretched wide.
Just as he is about to crash into a building or a
tree, he suddenly shoots back up into the sky.
Sometimes he dives so close to a building that the
gravel on the roof rattles.

Another bird that you can see in the city sky is the chimney swift. He is a little gray bird with a very short tail.

Chimneys on school buildings not used in the summer make good homes for these birds.

In the morning, they pour out of the chimneys, almost like smoke. They fly in every direction, twittering and chasing each other all over the sky. They never stop to rest once they leave their homes.

At night, they all return to their chimneys. They circle around in the air before they fly in to sleep.

Every evening in the summer, you can see purple martins, nighthawks and chimney swifts flying high over the rooftops. They dive and glide in the darkening sky, and catch tiny insects.

Near the end of summer, purple martins begin to gather from all parts of the city. They swarm on a tree or on telephone wires. Soon they will fly south for the winter.

Martins meet at the same time and place every year to begin their trip south. They sit together for hours twittering and fluttering about. Then suddenly they are gone!

The nighthawks with their strange calls are gone.
The chimney swifts that filled the summer sky,
and the robins who sang so sweetly are gone too.
Like the purple martins, these birds fly south for
the winter.

But the little sparrows stay on in the city. And so do the pigeons and starlings. They can be seen and heard even when the city is covered with snow.

ST. THOMAS SCHOOL